Quick 50 Guides

OVERLANDING AFRICA

50+ TIPS TO HELP YOU HAVE
THE TRIP OF A LIFETIME

CHRISTOPHER PERRY

OVERLANDING AFRICA
Copyright 2017 © Christopher Perry

Cover photo courtesy of Ginger Hilpipre

QUICK 50 GUIDES

Quick 50 guides have a simple aim: to provide practical and easy to follow tips that make a difference.

Our jargon free guides are written on the basis of first hand experience and our hope is that by passing on the tips we have learnt along the way, Quick 50 Guides will help you to have the best possible experiences first time around.

This book is the first of our Quick 50 Guides. For more information, and for upcoming titles, visit our website at www.quick50guides.com or find us on social media.

Instagram
Quick50guides

Twitter
@quick50guides

YouTube
Quick50guides

What is Overlanding?
And why should I do it?

Before we get started, it is worth taking a moment to explain what we actually mean by overlanding.

There are a wide variety of overlanding trips through Africa, but they all involve travelling in a group (usually between 10 – 30 people) with one or, more usually, two guides to help you along the way. Most of your travelling will be done in an overland vehicle, which will probably resemble something between a truck and a minibus, and you are likely to spend most of your nights in tents with the occasional night in a hostel or hotel.

It is my firmly held belief that overlanding is the best way to see a continent as large and diverse as Africa. By driving between the main points of interest you get the chance to see parts of Africa that you would never otherwise see, and it is a great way to challenge any pre-conceptions you may have of this amazing continent.

The back-to-basics approach provides a great sense of adventure but all the while you have the security of travelling with local experts and the safety in numbers of a large group.

Backpacking is the most popular way to travel in many parts of the world and whilst it is possible to backpack around Africa, the reality is that the infrastructure for travelling is not as developed in parts of Africa as it is in other regions of the world such as Europe or South America.

Overlanding takes away most of the stresses of planning a trip, and the tours' packed itineraries combined with the operators' relationships with locals make overlanding the best way to pack a lot into a relatively short space of time at a cheaper cost than you would otherwise have to pay if travelling on your own.

From the wonder of the Egyptian Pyramids to the beauty of Table Mountain via the plains of the Serengeti and the power of Victoria Falls, Africa is host to some of the world's most awe inspiring places.

Wherever you have travelled in the past, trust me on this one, overlanding through Africa will be the trip of a lifetime.

CONTENTS

PART I.
PLANNING YOUR TRIP

#1

FIND THE PERFECT TOUR FOR YOU

There are a wide variety of companies offering a whole host of different tours, and it is important to take the time right at the outset to make sure that you find the best trip for you.

Some of the factors you should consider when making your decision include:

- **Focus:** Wildlife, geography, beaches, cities… Different tours have different focuses. Have a think about what you most want to get out of your trip.
- **Target age group:** Some tours are targeted at specific age groups, think about whether one of these tours might work for you.
- **Itinerary:** Are there specific places you want to see?
- **Dates:** Not all tours are run regularly, find a tour that fits your preferred dates.
- **Budget:** The costs of overlanding tours can vary significantly, so find a tour that fits your budget.
- **Accommodation:** Whilst most accommodation on overlanding trips is fairly basic, there is some variation in accommodation options.

#2
DECIDE WHEN YOU WANT TO GO

Some travellers won't have flexibility in their dates, but if you do have flexibility then it is worth thinking about the best time to go as your experience in some parts of Africa will differ significantly depending on the season in which you visit.

Animal spotting is generally considered to be at its best in dry season, and you have the additional bonus of there being less chance of having to camp out in the rain. However there are benefits to the wet season too, as the luscious vegetation it brings can be stunningly beautiful.

One season is not clearly better than the other, it is just a matter of personal preference. This is well reflected by the differing experiences of Victoria Falls between wet and dry season. In dry season, you are able to get up close to the falls. For the Instagrammers amongst you dry season also provides you with the chance to go to Devil's Pool, the famous selfie spot at the top of the falls. Kayaking in the Zambezi is also at its most extreme in dry season. By contrast, in wet season the higher volume of water provides the opportunity to see the full might of Victoria Falls in all of its awe-inspiring glory.

Other things to consider are:

- If you are visiting the Serengeti or the Masai Mara, try to time your trip to catch the migration.
- Are there any specific events you want to catch? For example, the festival Afrika Burn now attracts festival-goers from all across the world.

#3

TAG ON A FEW DAYS AT EITHER END

Most of the overlanding trips in Africa start and finish in some pretty cool places and some, like Cape Town or Victoria Falls, might even be amongst the highlights of your trip.

However, often your tour's itinerary will not include more than half a day or so at these locations and as a result I strongly recommend that, if time and budget permits, you book a couple of extra nights at either end of the tour.

Going out a few days early has the added bonus of helping you to get comfortable in what is likely to be quite a different environment to home. There is also a good chance you will stumble across some of the other travellers who will be joining your tour and you can start making new friends before you have even got going. To save yourself the hassle of unpacking and packing, a ritual you will soon grow tired of, it is usually best to stay in the same accommodation where you will be joining your tour.

After the tour it can be great fun to explore your final destination with some of your new found friends, without the constraints of a rigid itinerary. Often people choose to stay in the same accommodation as the last night of the trip, but equally the temptation to stay somewhere slightly more luxurious is often too tempting for many to resist.

And a final word of warning... if you are starting or finishing in Cape Town then a few days might not be enough!

#4

SET A REALISTIC BUDGET

Budgeting can be one of the most difficult aspects of planning a trip to Africa. As well as the basic cost of the trip and flights, other costs to factor in include:

- Visas;
- Vaccinations/Medication/Malaria Tablets;
- Any new equipment or clothes you might need for your trip;
- Money for optional activities which are not included in the price of your tour;
- Travel insurance (a requirement by most tour operators);
- Spending money;
- Souvenirs;

And ...

#5

DON'T FORGET TO FACTOR IN TIPS

One of the costs that travellers often forget to factor in is tips. On your trip you will have at least one guide/driver, although most trips have two.

It is generally expected that you will tip your guide at the end of your trip and whilst the amount you tip is obviously at your discretion, the guideline for tipping given by tour operators is usually along the lines of US$2/3 per day.

You are also likely to do activities with local operators, and it is customary for travellers to tip those local operators too.

#6

GET YOUR VACCINATIONS

AND MEDICATION SORTED EARLY

A few months before travelling you should check in with your local doctor about what vaccinations and other medication you might need for the trip. Go to your appointment armed with details of the places you are visiting so that you can get advice specifically tailored to your trip.

It is particularly important to check whether you require yellow fever vaccinations, as a valid yellow fever certificate is an entry requirement for some African countries.

Some vaccinations take a while to become effective, and others require a course of several injections over a period of weeks or months, so you need to start getting the inoculations in plenty of time.

Similarly, if you need to take malaria tablets, you also will often have to start taking them four weeks or more ahead of your trip so you need to get these sorted ahead of time.

#7

IDENTIFY YOUR VISA REQUIREMENTS

Many of the African countries along the popular overlanding routes require travellers to obtain visas prior to entry.

You need to thoroughly research which visas you need to acquire, and how to obtain them.

Whilst the popular approach is to get as many visas for your trip as possible on the borders of their respective countries, it is important to note that for certain nationalities at certain borders this will not be an option so you need to have done your research beforehand. There is plenty of guidance online as to visas requirements or you can always contact the embassy of each country who should be able to give you guidance as to the best approach.

#8

MAKE SURE YOUR PASSPORT IS IN ORDER

Before travelling you should make sure you have plenty of time until the expiry of you passport, with 6 months after the intended end of your trip as an absolute minimum.

You also need to make sure you have plenty of empty pages, as some countries require a minimum of two empty pages in your passport to allow you to enter.

It is sensible to take a copy of your passport with you on your trip in case something happens to the original, just make sure you keep it separate from your passport.

PART II.
WHAT TO TAKE

#9

IF IT'S A MAYBE – DON'T TAKE IT

The aim of packing for this sort of trip is always to pack everything you need, but at the same to have to carry as light a load as possible in your bag.

The reality of packing for these sorts of trips is that however hard you try, you will probably end up taking a few things that you never use and that there will be a few things that you end up wishing you had packed.

If this is your first trip of this kind, then you are more likely to over pack than under pack, so I suggest you use the rule of thumb that if it's a maybe – don't take it!

Bonus Tip: Clothing

When deciding what clothes to take have a look at the climate for the areas and time of year that you are visiting. You should also:

- Not take any clothes you don't mind getting ruined by dust and dirt (white clothes are a particularly bad idea!);
- Take some neutral coloured clothes if you are going on safari; and
- Take some clothes to cover your arms and lengths – to provide respite from both sun and mosquitos.

#10

CHOOSE THE RIGHT BAG

Choosing the right bag for your trip will make your life a lot easier. The rigidity of a suitcase is unsuited to being stored in the back of an overland vehicle, yet alone spending the night in a crowded tent so leave your suitcase at home, and take either a backpack or a duffel bag. Ideally the bag you take should be waterproof, or at the very least water resistant.

If you take a backpack, it is useful to have one that you can open from the front as well as the top – to save you having to unpack the whole bag to find that one item which has inevitably fallen to the bottom.

You should also give some thought as to what day bag you are taking. There may be occasions on your trip when you live out of your day pack for a few days – so make sure it is up to the task!

#11

PACKING CUBES WILL MAKE YOUR LIFE EASIER

You will spend a lot of time on your trip packing and unpacking your bag, and packing cubes are a great way to save yourself a lot of time and frustration.

You can use packing cubes to compartmentalise your bag, using separate cubes for underwear, t-shirts, medicine etc. It will save you from frantically rooting around in your bag at 5:30 in the morning looking for the one thing you desperately need whilst the rest of your group sit in the overland vehicle waiting for you. Trust me on this, it's a situation you would rather avoid.

You can buy packing cubes from most luggage shops or from plenty of places online.

#12

TAKE A SUITABLE SLEEPING BAG

Do some research as to what the climate will be like during your trip. Don't be fooled into thinking it will always be scorchingly hot, as temperatures can drop steeply at night and you don't want to end up struggling to sleep because you are too cold. So find out what the temperature will be like, and then take a sleeping bag suited to those temperatures.

I also recommend taking a sleeping bag liner. Not only are they comfortable to sleep in, but they also give you the flexibility that if it gets too hot for a sleeping bag you can sleep in just the liner.

#13

PACK A COMFY PILLOW

Once your sleeping bag is sorted, the next thing you need to sort is a pillow. Don't be tempted to make do with rolling up clothes or using your bag, a comfy pillow is a must. Blow up pillows are practical but not particularly comfortable. Travel roll-up fabric pillows are a more comfortable option – or you can even go for one of each.

Large parts of the long days of driving are usually spent trying to catch up on the sleep you missed out on from late nights and early mornings, so you should also take a travel neck pillow for the long hours on the road.

#14

BE PREPARED TO WASH AS YOU GO

Unless you are going on a short trip, you probably won't pack enough clothes to last for its duration so you will have to do some washing as you go along.

Whilst at some of your accommodation there might be a basic laundry service on offer, you should be prepared to do your own washing as you go along. To make life easier, you should take:

- eco-friendly travel washing liquid/powder;
- a universal sink plug adaptor; and
- a washing line.

It is also worth packing a waterproof dry bag. There might be occasions when you have to pack you bag and some of the clothes you washed the night before have not quite dried. Putting these clothes in a separate bag will avoid getting the rest of your clothes damp.

#15

TAKE THE BEST CAMERA YOU CAN...

Wherever you have travelled before, you will see things on your overland trip through Africa that will blow you away.

Whilst your focus should always be on soaking up every new experience, it's a shame not to be able to take some photos to jog your memory in the years to come. A video recorder is also a great way of being able to capture moments throughout your trip.

Particularly when it comes to photographing animals, the better the camera the better the photo so take the best camera with you that you possibly can. It is relatively common for travellers to use a trip through Africa as an excuse to treat themselves to a new camera, and if you can do so then great! However, cameras can be expensive so if you can't afford a new one then think about whether any of your friends or family would be willing to lend you one (just make sure you get it covered by your insurance before you go) or look into renting one for a slightly more cost-friendly alternative to buying one.

If all else fails you can always use your smartphone camera looking down the lens of a pair of binoculars, a trick which, with a bit of practice, can work surprisingly well.

#16

...AND LEARN HOW IT WORKS BEFORE YOU GO

Sitting in the back of a jeep watching a pride of lions on the hunt is not the time to be familiarising yourself with your camera settings. So take a bit of time before your trip to improve your understanding of your camera. It is even worth practising by trying to take some photos of your own local wildlife.

The first photos I took of wild rhinos came out so bright that it looked like I had taken the photos only moments before an asteroid struck earth. So don't make the same mistakes I did.

#17

A BATTERY CHARGER PACK PREVENTS STRESS

There may be occasions on your trip, particularly when you are bush camping, when you will go at least a day or two without access to mains electricity.

This can be a problem, as those days are often the highlights of the trip, and will be when you use your camera the most (think Serengeti, Okovango Delta etc.)

The simple solution is to take a battery charging pack. The technology has come a long way in recent years and you can now buy a pack that will charge your devices many times over pretty cheaply, and more importantly it won't take up much room in your bag.

It's just another way to make sure you don't miss out on the perfect photo!

#18

TAKE A SPARE MEMORY CARD

If you do take a good camera with you, the likelihood is that you will end up taking hundreds if not thousands of photographs. Taking photographs of animals can be tricky, so you will probably take lots of photos that end up being deleted. Whilst some of the deleting can happen as you go along, you still want to make sure that you have plenty of memory to hold all of your photographs so it is worth taking a spare memory card to avoid the dreaded "memory full" message.

Bonus Tip: Backing up your photos

If possible it is worth taking something to back up your photos. You can get memory card adaptors for tablets, or you can even take a small laptop to store your photos. If you don't have a way to back up your photos, try to distribute your photos over a few memory cards to minimise the risk of losing all of your photos.

#19

BE PREPARED FOR THE MOSQUITOS

There are areas of Africa where mosquitos are an unfortunate part of everyday life. While it would be a miracle to pass through some of the worst effected areas without getting bitten, a good quality insect repellent gives you the best chance of minimising the damage.

I recommend taking one with a high deet level, they smell unpleasant but they are the most effective at keeping the bugs away. Surprisingly, the repellents sold locally in Africa are often not particularly strong, so you would be better off taking your own strong repellent with you.

You should also pack some anti-itch cream to treat any bites you do receive.

#20

TAKE A FEW MEDICAL SUPPLIES

The one area where the "if it's a maybe – don't take it" rule shouldn't be applied, is where it comes to packing a few basic medical supplies.

As cautious as you try to be, there is still a chance that you will get an upset stomach on your trip and it is better to be prepared for the worst case-scenario. So take some anti-diahorea tablets along with you, as well as some re-hydration tablets.

It is also worth taking some pain killers as well as a basic first aid kit containing plasters, bandages, anti-sceptic etc.

#21

PROVIDE YOUR OWN ENTERTAINMENT

Whilst your trip will be full of amazing experiences, you will have time to kill both on long travelling days in the overland vehicle and in the evenings at the campsites.

For travelling days, factor in the "African massage" provided by the varying quality of African roads which makes music, podcasts and audiobooks all good options. For those less prone to travel sickness books, crosswords/sudokus, films and TV series are also popular.

To pass the time in the evenings, a pack of playing cards or uno cards are a great way to socialise by the campfire.

One of the great aspects of overlanding is that it brings together people from across the world. Campfires are a great place to share stories and to get to know each other. By the end of the trip you might even feel like you know more about some of your fellow travellers than you do some of your friends from home.

#22

TAKE A STURDY PAIR OF SHOES

Packing the right shoes for your trip takes some thought. Lots of travellers take both trainers and walking boots, but the best option is to take walking shoes which are halfway between the two. Whatever shoes you take, make sure they are well worn in as you do not want to be dealing with blisters on your trip.

A robust pair of flip flops is also a must.

#23

CHANGE THINGS UP WITH

A SET OF DRESSIER CLOTHES

Let's face it, you probably won't be winning any fashion awards during your trip through Africa. Practicality should be prioritised over style and you really don't need to worry about looking your best.

That being said, it is worth taking one slightly dressier set of clothes on your trip with you. In some of the towns you visit there will be the opportunity to go to a restaurant for a nicer dinner or to go for a night out in the local bars and clubs and on those evenings it is nice to have the option to wear something slightly smarter.

#24

A HEAD TORCH CAN BE A LIFE SAVER

The nature of most tours means that you will often be going to sleep after the sun sets and will regularly have to pack up your belongings and your tent before the sun rises again. A head torch will make your life much easier by leaving you with both your hands free for the task at hand. They are also handy for any late night toilet trips.

You should also remember to pack some spare batteries.

#25

US DOLLARS ARE ALWAYS HANDY

It is worth taking a supply of US Dollars with you on your trip. Local ATMs can be unreliable, but it is usually possible to find somewhere to exchange dollars for local currency. Often it is not even necessary to exchange your dollars, lots of restaurants and shops will accept US Dollars, and it is also usually possible to pay for optional activities in dollars.

A word of warning, when getting your dollars you should ensure they are all in good condition and dated post 2006, otherwise you run the risk of the notes being rejected.

#26

ITEMS FOR LOCALS

GUARANTEE A WARM WELCOME

Many of the overlanding tours include opportunities to visit local communities and provide a chance to get a better understanding of people's lives. The visits will often include a visit to a local school. A great way to guarantee a friendly welcome is to take along stationary such as pens and notebooks for the school to use. These items are usually in short supply and will be gratefully received. Balloons are also a great way to bring a smile to the local children's faces.

PART III.
ON THE ROAD

#27

GET STUCK IN

Overlanding Africa trips are fully participatory, which means that whilst the emphasis is on you having fun – you will also be expected to help out to ensure that the trip runs smoothly. There will usually be a rota dividing up the daily chores, which might include:

- Cooking;
- Washing up;
- Packing/unpacking the vehicle;
- Cleaning the inside of the vehicle; and
- Cleaning the campsite.

You should always make sure you pull your weight, and don't be the one who always disappears to the showers when its their turn to wash up. If everyone mucks in then the system works really well, but if people start to slack then it can cause frustration.

I strongly advocate going beyond the duties you are assigned. For example, when you are having a roadside lunch give the cooking team an extra pair of hands – all you will otherwise be doing is sitting watching them cook and by helping you will get to eat your lunch quicker.

By the same token, if you have finished putting up your tent see if anyone else needs a hand putting up theirs. Your help will probably be gratefully received, and when it comes to your turn to need some help in the future then it is more likely to be forthcoming.

#28

GO WITH THE FLOW

There may well be times on your trip when things don't go entirely to plan. The relaxed attitudes of locals, changeable weather and encounters with animals are just some of the things that make Africa an exciting place to travel but are the same things that can cause frustration.

When things don't go quite to plan, try to take it in your stride and think of it as part of the experience. Besides, more often than not, the times when things go slightly wrong turn out to the best stories to tell at the end of your trip.

#29

EMBRACE EVERY OPPORTUNITY

My approach to these sorts of trips is to always do all I can to avoid having any regrets at the end of the trip. The last thing you want to be thinking about when you return to your daily life is that one activity you wished you had done. I understand that some of the optional activities on an overlanding trip, like hot air balloon rides or skydiving, can be quite expensive but do all you can to get the most out of the budget you have. You could also ask friends and family to replace any birthday/Christmas presents with contributions towards any of the optional activities you have your eyes on.

You should also make sure that you make the most of any free optional activities on offer: it always amazes me the number of people who don't. If you get the chance to sleep out under the stars – take it! It will be an unforgettable experience. If you get the chance to swim in an abandoned hippo pool in the Okovango Delta – then give it a go! These are the sort of experiences that will stay with you long after you have left Africa.

#30
MAKE FRIENDS WITH YOUR GUIDE

The most valuable resource on your trip will be your guide(s). Not only are they responsible for getting you safely to your destination, they should also be a goldmine of information along the way.

Every guide is different, but they should all have enough knowledge to be able to give you a deeper understanding of the places you go and the people you meet.

They can also be a great source of advice on, amongst other things:

- Restaurants to try;
- Which optional activities to prioritise;
- What to pack in your day bag for the next day; and
- What shoes to wear on a given day.

The guides will often have great anecdotes from previous trips that can make brilliant campfire stories and many of the guides also have fascinating life stories to share with you if you show an interest.

#31

DRINK PLENTY OF WATER

When people start to feel unwell on an overloading trip, it is often because they are dehydrated. It is important to keep drinking water, even if you don't feel thirsty. Try to ensure you always have access to 2 litres of water and drink regularly throughout the day.

You always need to be sure that the water you are drinking is safe. The safest approach is to drink bottled water. This is unfortunately not very environmentally friendly, so try to buy the large 5 litre bottles to minimise waste. It is worth holding onto the bottles you do use, as they can be given to local communities for collecting and storing water.

Your overland vehicle may have its own water tank on board containing drinking water, which provides a cheaper and more environmentally friendly alternative but be warned that the treatment used to purify the water can make it taste slightly unpleasant.

Check with your guide before drinking any water out of a tap and if the water is unsafe to drink, then you should also avoid using it to clean your teeth as any harmful bacteria could still find their way into your system.

#32

ESTABLISH A MALARIA TABLET ROUTINE

Malaria tablets are a necessary evil during most trips to Africa. You have probably heard the horror stories of the pills' nasty side effects, but the reality is that the pills are a necessary evil and could save your life.

You should seek out your doctor's advice as to which pills to take, and how they should be taken but when it comes to your trip it is important to remember to actually take them!

For smartphone users, I recommend downloading one of the many medication apps available. These apps can be set up to send you numerous reminder notifications over a certain period of time everyday that will hopefully help to prevent you from forgetting.

#33

LEARN TO DO YOUR TENT PROPERLY

Part of your daily routine on an overland trip will be putting your tent up in the evening and taking out down in the morning. It is not an aspect of the trip that many people relish but, with a bit of practice, there is no reason why it shouldn't be a pretty painless process.

The first night you spend in the tents you should ask your guide to demonstrate the best way to take the tent up and put it down, although most guides should volunteer to do so without you asking.

Even if you have done plenty of camping in the past, the chances are there will be some particular quirks to the tents you are using on your trip. If you can get the technique nailed down, then it will give you a chance of beating the shower queue (on the days there are showers) in the evenings, and more importantly a few extra minutes of sleep in the mornings.

Bonus Tip: Zip up your tent

Whenever your tent is set up you should keep it fully zipped up to try and prevent mosquitos from getting inside. It will also keep out snakes and other animals, the last thing you want to find when you get back to your tent late at night is an unwanted guest!

#34
ACCEPT THE LACK OF INTERNET

One of the many joys of a trip through Africa is the feeling that you are escaping everyday life, and for better or worse that includes leaving behind many of the modern technologies.

Internet coverage is pretty sparse across large parts of Africa, so the chances are there will be periods where you will go for days at a time without connection. Even where there is internet, there is a good chance that once you try to connect there will turn out to be a maddeningly bad connection.

You are better off accepting the lack of internet from the outset, and then viewing any internet you do manage to connect to as a bonus. Try to see the lack of internet as a lack of distraction, giving you the best chance of soaking up all the incredible experiences you are having.

#35

DON'T FEED THE ANIMALS

Unless explicitly told otherwise, please don't feed the animals you encounter on your trip. This may seem like common sense, but plenty of people still get it wrong.

When interacting with wild animals, it is difficult to predict how they might react to being offered food and some animals, most noticably baboons, can become very aggressive. Offering wild animals food will also encourage them to become reliant on humans, which could cause other issues further down the line.

It is not uncommon for campsites to have dogs or other pets. I also discourage you from feeding these animals. The pets may have specific dietary requirements that you are unaware of, and so feeding the pet could actually be endangering its health.

#36

TREAT THE LOCALS WITH RESPECT

Throughout your trip you will come across locals from a wide variety of backgrounds and cultures. It is important that you treat them all with respect, even if there are aspects of their cultures that you disagree with.

There are some places where you may need to modify how you dress to conform to cultural expectations. For example, Stone Town on the island of Zanzibar is a majority Muslim city and as such appropriate clothing will need to be worn. Your guide should give you plenty of warning if you are entering such an area, as well as give you advice as to what is appropriate.

It is also important that you ask a person's permission before you take a photo of them. I am sure you would find it quite intrusive if a stranger took a photo of you as you went about your daily life, and it is no different in Africa. Asking beforehand minimises the risk of any bad feeling and in my experience it is pretty rare for someone to say no. If they do say yes, then offer to show them the photo on your camera's screen once you have taken it as the locals will often really enjoy seeing their photos.

#37

BE RESPECTFUL OF OTHER TRAVELLERS

There will be other travellers on your trip, and for the duration of your adventure you will be living in close proximity to each other.

This proximity helps to forge close bonds, and lasting friendships are often formed on overlanding trips. The flip side is that there may be people on your trip who you don't get on with quite so well. It is important to treat everyone on your trip with respect, and to try to avoid gossiping which can create tension in the group. Think of it as a way to develop your diplomacy skills, as well as your tolerance levels!

It is particularly important to be mindful of other travellers at night. If you are staying up late at night chatting to friends and/or listening to music, try to make sure you are doing so in a way that minimises the impact on anyone who has already gone to their tent to get some sleep.

A special effort should be made if you are sharing a tent with someone you had not met before the tour. You will come to rely on each other when it comes to setting up/taking down your tent and you will spend a lot of time together, so things will run much smoother if you get on well.

You should also take extra care when handling other people's belongings.

#38

BUSHY BUSHY WILL BECOME A PART OF DAILY LIFE

One of the less glamorous aspects of travelling through Africa, is the toilet situation. Whilst there will be normal toilets to use along your trip, there will also be occasions where you don't have access to one.

There will be times, whether by the side of the road or at a remote campsite, where you won't have access to a toilet and a bush will have to do. This is often affectionately known as "bushy bushy".

The exercise is obviously easier for males, but it is something both sexes get used to pretty quickly, and isn't actually as bad as you are probably imagining. You just need to be careful when you are heading into the bush that there are no unpleasant surprises waiting for you and remember to take some toilet paper and hand sanitizer with you.

If you need to leave your tent at night to go to the toilet then you need to be careful. You should take a torch with you and check for any eyes reflecting the light back at you. In some of the more remote campsites it might even be worth asking your tent buddy to go with you.

#39

KEEP A TRAVEL DIARY

The sad reality is that memories fade over time, and whilst photos are a great way of capturing a moment they often fail to tell the full story.

That's why I think it really is worth taking the time to keep a travel journal over the course of your trip. There will be plenty of time on the long journeys and evenings at campsites, so you don't have any excuses.

It doesn't have to be pages of immaculately written prose, just enough to be able to look back upon in the years to come and jog your memory about all the incredible experiences you had.

#40

TRY TO LEARN A FEW WORDS
IN EACH LOCAL LANGUAGE

A great way to bring a smile to the locals you meet is to speak a few words of the local language.

Now I'm not proposing you become an expert, or even take up language lessons - the best thing to do is to simply ask your guide to teach you a few words in the local language each time you cross a border and enter a new country.

To get you started, here are a few of the basic Swahili phrases (a language used in most East African countries):

- Jambo – Hello;
- Tafadhali – Please;
- Asante – Thank You;
- Ndiyo – Yes; and
- Hapana – No.

#41

PLAY BY THE FRIDGE RULES

Most overland vehicles have a fridge for the communal use of the travellers. The fridge is usually used to store snacks, alcohol and other drinks and can be really handy as long as everyone treats the fridge with respect, but it can also be a source of frustration.

The most common problem arises where people take something from the fridge that isn't theirs which, although usually by accident, can cause resentment. An easy way to avoid this is to use a marker pen to write your name on anything you put in the fridge and to just be careful when you are taking something out of it.

If you put any perishable food items in the fridge then make sure you don't forget about them. Mouldy food can present a health risk and will also make the fridge stink!

It is also important to make sure that any liquids you put in the fridge are properly sealed. Causing a flood in the fridge and covering everyone's stuff in a sticky liquid is a quick way to make yourself slightly less popular.

#42

SUPPORT LOCAL BUSINESSES WHERE YOU CAN

On your trip there will be plenty of opportunities to buy souvenirs. When deciding which ones to buy, I think you should consider not just what you are buying but also who you are buying it from.

In some tourist shops it can be hard to identify what is a genuine locally produced product, and what is a cheaply produced imitation.

As a result, you should look to buy your souvenirs from places where it is clear how the products have been manufactured.

From social enterprises employing local people living with disabilities to companies reinvesting sale proceeds into fighting poaching, there are a host of brilliant businesses that sell high quality souvenirs and also do valuable work in their communities that you can support.

If you buy from any of these businesses, in the future your souvenir will not only remind you of your trip but also of how you supported a local community when you bought it.

#43

BUT DON'T BE AFRAID TO HAGGLE

When shopping for souvenirs you should be wary of the fact that the initial price offered to you will normally be an inflated one. Do not be embarrassed to haggle, the seller will be expecting it.

Make an offer below what you would actually be prepared to pay and you will usually end up at a fair price.

#44

PROTECT YOURSELF FROM THE SUN

Don't underestimate the power of the African sun. Everyone wants to go home after a trip through Africa with a pretty impressive tan but unless you live in a similar climate the likelihood is your skin won't be used to the intensity of the sun's rays. Take some reasonable strength sun cream and diligently reapply it, particularly during the middle of the day when the sun is at its most powerful.

When it comes to sunbathing, limit yourself to short sharp bursts. However much sun cream you put on, if you spend too long exposing your skin to the sun then the chances are you will get burnt and neither a tent nor an overland truck are particularly forgiving places to be dealing with sunburn. If you are travelling on your own don't be embarrassed to ask someone else on the trip to help you apply suncream to your back, they are probably looking for someone to do the same for them!

It's also a good idea to wear a hat when you are out in the sun, to try and protect yourself from sunstroke.

#45

BE CAREFUL WITH YOUR VALUABLES

As when travelling through any part of the world, you need to be careful with your valuables to try to avoid anything going missing.

Most overland vehicles have an on-board safe which you should use to store your passport, credit cards and other valuables.

When you are out and about you should avoid keeping your cash in a wallet or purse, and instead use a money belt. Money belts can be concealed easily under your clothes and are also secured around your waist. If you have an expensive camera, it is worth keeping it in a bag and out of view when in densely populated areas.

You should keep a lock on your bag, but avoid putting a lock on your tent zipper as it is only likely to make your tent a target.

#46
TREAT ATMs WITH CAUTION

ATMs can be a source of frustration in some parts of Africa, due to the relatively frequent unavailability of cash. Try to avoid a situation where you have completely run out of cash as it could be a while before you are able to withdraw more money. Try to plan ahead and start to look for a cashpoint while you still have some funds to keep you going.

ATMs can be particularly problematic in Zimbabwe where the availability of cash is tightly controlled to manage the risk of inflation which has previously crippled the country's economy. It is therefore advisable to have some US dollars prior to entering the country.

ATMs at border crossings are also unreliable, and you should try to make sure you have any required cash before you arrive at the border.

When using an ATM be mindful of who is around you, and avoid counting your cash out in the open.

#47

BE PREPARED FOR BORDER CROSSINGS

African border crossings can be a frustrating experience and it will often take several hours for an entire group to make the crossing.

The crossing will usually be a two part process, as you will first be stamped out of the country you are leaving and will then be stamped into the new country.

Although delays are sometimes inevitable when travelling as part of a large group, there are things you can do to make your own border crossing as painless as possible:

- Know your visa requirements ahead of time. (See tip #7 for more advice);
- Have a pen to hand. Most border crossings require forms to be filled in, and pens are usually in short supply;
- Know details relevant to your stay in the new country including what accommodation you will be staying at, the length of stay in that country and your vehicle's registration number; and
- If you are paying for your visa on arrival, make sure you have the requisite cash well in advance as ATMs at border crossings are notoriously unreliable.

#48

TRY LOCAL DELICACIES WHERE YOU CAN

African cuisine is incredibly diverse and will give you the chance to taste foods that you might not otherwise get the chance to try. Be open minded when it comes to trying things, and you might discover a new favourite dish! Things to look out for include:

- Red bananas in Tanzania;
- Game steak such as Springbok, Kudu and Oryx;
- Kilimanjaro beer;
- South African wine; and
- Biltong.

#49

GIVE YOUR FEEDBACK

Once your tour is over, the tour company will usually ask you to fill in a feedback form (either by handing out a physical form or sending a link to an online form).

It really is worth you taking the time to fill out the form honestly, as the tour operator can then use your feedback to improve the tour for future travellers. It is also an important way for the companies to monitor the performance of their guides so you should pay particular attention to this part of the form.

#50

ENJOY IT!

An overlanding trip through Africa is an adventure of a lifetime. You will meet some great people and experience some incredible things. Have an awesome time!

When you are home from your trip come and tell us about it at www.quick50guides.com and share any tips of your own!

22561371R00038

Printed in Great Britain
by Amazon